ALSO BY ROBERT DE GAST

The Doors of San Miguel de Allende

Five Fair Rivers

Unreal Estate

The Lighthouses of the Chesapeake

Western Wind, Eastern Shore

The Oystermen of the Chesapeake

The
Churches
and
Chapels
of
San Miguel
de Allende

The Churches and Chapels of San Miguel de Allende

Robert de Gast

E&R Publications   Birdsnest, VA

Published by E&R Publications, Box 32, Birdsnest, VA 23307 USA

ISBN 0-9655420-0-9

Designed by Nancy Gallagher

First Edition

Printed in Hong Kong

For Evelyn, always

Acknowledgements

Many people made this book possible. Some helped me find chapels or locate obscure information. Others helped physically, financially, spiritually. I thank especially: Luis Felipe Nieto, Liliane Maya, James Olsen, Barry Shapiro, Evelyn de Gast, Tony Cohan, Joan Palmer, Jaime Fernández Harris, César del Río García, Héctor Ulloa, Gary Driver, Eduardo and Micaela Obregón, Sareda Milosz, Rogelio Flores, Lauro Antonio Fernández, Roy Sorrels, John and Barbara Clum, Jane Evans, Joyce and Morton Stith, Lies Wiegman, Donna Meyer, R.P. Saturnino Tovar Murillo, Nancy Gallagher, Richard Anderson, Stirling Dickinson, Katie Burke, Dianne Kushner, Ken Coburn, Glorian Dorsey, David and Sabrina Glaeser, Marc Winderman, George Trask, Allie Eilers, Juan Manuel Fajardo Orozco, Ana Cristina Guerrero and the many *campesinos* in the *ranchos* whose names I'll never know.

PREFACE

*Churches, everywhere churches . . . San Miguel abounds in churches,
all interesting and many quite beautiful.*

- Alice Adams
Mexico: Some Travels and Some Travelers There

I t is impossible not to be aware of churches and chapels in San
Miguel de Allende. The most prominent buildings, as in most
Mexican communities, are the religious ones. Before arriving in
town the first-time visitor is likely to have seen the pink, drip-castle-
like principal church called simply "La Parroquia," the parish church.
That enchanting edifice, reproduced on a myriad of postcards, travel
posters, and tourist brochures, is the icon that announces San Miguel
the way the Eiffel Tower says Paris, or the Golden Gate Bridge heralds
San Francisco.

On my first visit to San Miguel ten years ago I remember
using La Parroquia to get my bearings; I could nearly always see its
spires wherever I was, and not feel lost. The fact that La Parroquia
fronts the Jardín, the central plaza of town, the "living room" of the
community, also made it the homing device of choice. Like everyone
else I was seduced into taking pictures of it. I've been making photographs of the churches of San Miguel ever since.

Although, heaven knows, there were many other ecclesiastical points of reference, and as on subsequent visits I became acquaint-
ed with this pretty city, I discovered exactly what Alice Adams meant:
there seemed to be no limit. Only a few blocks from the Jardín stands
the religious complex of the Church of San Francisco and the Church
of the Third Order; the Church and Convent of La Concepción; and a

block-long gathering of several churches facing the Plaza Cívica. As I became used to the 6,300 foot altitude and increased the range of my walking excursions, I made many more discoveries: the charming chapel of San José on the way to Los Balcones; the two tiny chapels, still in use, in the neighborhood called Las Cuevitas; the abandoned (and ruined) remains of the little but grandly named Oratorio de las Siete Dolores de la Santísima Virgen above the waterworks at El Chorro; the imposing churches in the neighborhoods of San Juan de Dios and San Antonio; more than three dozen churches and chapels, all within easy walking distance of La Parroquia.

During one of my more ambitious hikes, past the railroad station into the outlying countryside, I stumbled upon the heartbreakingly beautiful chapel of San Miguel Viejo near the original settlement of San Miguel. Although little more than two miles from the center of town, it is centuries removed in time.

During a stay in late fall after the rainy season, I also had a chance to canoe on the presa, the reservoir just outside of the city, where I discovered the steeple of the chapel of the Hacienda of Agustín González, inundated when the reservoir was constructed in 1967. Only a few feet of the steeple showed. In more recent years even the base of the chapel has been completely exposed on many occasions, the result of a vexing and continuing drought.

Like most new residents, and nearly all tourists, I didn't have an automobile during my first visits to San Miguel. It was therefore an unusual opportunity when my friends Barbara and John Clum invited my wife and me on a sightseeing tour of the countryside in their four-wheel drive vehicle. In less than thirty minutes, and within a half dozen miles from town, we had forded a river, driven some of the worst dirt roads I'd ever been on, and happened upon five intriguing chapels, three of them apparently abandoned. The Clums told us of many more scattered in the campo around San Miguel. I had no idea that there were other "country" chapels. But from that moment on I was on what we came to call "a steeplechase."

When eventually we brought a car to San Miguel I learned firsthand about those roads. Although there are hundreds of miles of trails, burro-and-goat-paths, and many more miles of unpaved roads, there are less than a hundred miles of paved roads in the country outside the town of San Miguel. Those are the highways leading south to Celaya, east to Querétaro, north to Dolores Hidalgo, and west to Guanajuato. They are two-lane asphalt roads, often in poor condition, usually without center stripes, always without shoulders. The dirt roads are, by and large, mere rutted paths. In the rainy season (from June to October) many become impassable, even for cars or trucks with four-wheel drive.

Nevertheless, it is possible, most of the time, to drive to nearly every active village chapel. The priests who serve mass do so once or twice a month. But many of the abandoned chapels can now only be reached on foot, sometimes as much as an hour's walk from the nearest road.

There are, of course, thousands and thousands of churches scattered throughout the Republic of Mexico. I decided to concentrate my treasure hunt on the *municipio* of San Miguel de Allende, one of 46 such municipalities in the State of Guanajuato (and one of 2,412 such "counties" in Mexico).

The first difficulty was to locate the municipal limits. The location of the borders of the map I obtained from the San Miguel Public Works department varied to some extent with the topographic maps I found at INEGI, Mexico's Geographic Institute, but since the areas in question were in very mountainous terrain, no churches were there anyway. In any event, the borders remain a surveyor's nightmare: apparently not a straight line exists for more than a few hundred yards!

The discrepancies of the municipal limits were nothing compared with the errors within the maps themselves. Commercial

Mexican road maps are notoriously unreliable, and even the (quite beautiful) government topographic maps are riddled with flagrant errors. Since the topo maps are rather dated (1970), few of the recently hard-surfaced roads are shown. Spelling errors were often confusing: San Juan de Gracia turned out to be San Juan de García — and vice versa — two different communities many miles apart. Some villages shown simply didn't exist; others were not where the map indicated they might be. The duplication of place-names was boggling. There were many places with identical names, only sometimes distinguished by antecedents like Arriba (Upper) or Abajo (Lower). But after some time, and much exploration, I was able to make some sense out of all this, correct the maps, and even amplify on the information, since I could notate the location of chapels that I discovered, often abandoned, in areas not near any existing settlement.

San Miguel de Allende occupies almost 600 square miles, only five percent of the area of the State of Guanajuato, a mostly hilly, occasionally mountainous, semi-desert area. Since the town of San Miguel is quite centrally located within the municipio, the farthest distance to any of its borders is no more than about 20 miles, and no church or chapel is more than about a dozen miles from La Parroquia . . . as the crow flies. Still, driving, the journey might take more than an hour.

I also soon discovered that there were a lot of new chapels, the result of the incredible population increase in Mexico in the last forty years, nearly tripling from 34 million in 1960 to an estimated 100 million by the end of the century. Most of these chapels in the new settlements and suburbs are unfinished, due more to financial factors rather than because of time.

My search for information led me to many sources. I obtained a list of the schools, reasoning that a place with a school might also have a chapel. I talked to soft-drink delivery truck drivers, thinking that where there were places to buy Coca-Cola there might be churches. I began to think of these delivery men as latter-day Franciscans:

they went everywhere. I talked to priests, obtained schedules of masses, thereby locating all active churches. And then I began systematic search expeditions in the campo.

My first attempts were by car, a low-slung Toyota sedan we had owned for some years. During the dry months it forged its way to a number of chapels but it soon became apparent that it would not be able to survive the rugged terrain. I located a 20-year old Chevrolet pickup truck and put new tires on it, hoping to make it equal to the task. The truck had Mexican plates and looked sufficiently disreputable to pass for a local vehicle. I was often able to offer rides, especially to people carrying heavy burdens. Sometimes these hitchhikers were able to show me an abandoned church I might otherwise have missed. From time to time the cab of the truck made an excellent high platform for photography, and the back of the truck made it possible, at times, to peek over a churchyard wall. Ringing the church bell usually brought the *mayordomo*, who would open the atrium or the chapel for a few pesos.

Many of the buildings could only be reached after a long walk. I would sometimes find myself totally lost while still literally in sight of San Miguel, fully aware of compass directions, but unable to find the "main" road again. "*¿Dónde estoy?*" — Where am I? — always brought a smile and sometimes a new chapel into my growing inventory. Twice I employed a "guide" to lead me to locations I could never have discovered by myself short of an aerial survey, but just as often the discovery was serendipitous and the result of many hours of dogged persistence.

Although I spent much time in very desolate, sparsely populated areas I never found myself fearful, except for dogs that might become fiercely protective while I was walking around a village taking photographs. I soon learned that in Mexico, where stones are always readily available, I only had to *pretend* to pick one up to make them scatter and retreat.

I was treated, without exception, with great courtesy and unfailing politeness, and was extended real hospitality. Villagers were delighted and proud to show me their church. But asking directions was always fraught with potential problems, and not only because of my halting Spanish. A curious bit of Mexican culture came into play: disliking admitting they don't know where something is, and to please the questioner (and themselves), people will make up directions to imaginary destinations. I quickly learned not to ask leading questions. Instead of saying, "The church is that way, right?" I would ask, "Is there a church near here?" And I found that I had to add adjectives like "old," "abandoned," or "in ruins," for unless I covered the specific description the answers might be very misleading. Asking women, especially older women, was a surer bet than asking men or children. I learned to say, "It's okay if you don't know." Sometimes I'd turn back to town in frustration, only to discover later that I'd come within a few hundred yards of an abandoned building hidden behind a clump of trees in the woods.

Every rancho may have a soccer-field, a school or two, electricity, possibly a well, but it will definitely have a chapel. And almost every chapel has a bell tower, a *campanario*, and at least one bronze bell, although it may be hung in a tree or suspended from a clothesline.

As my interest in the chapels became known in San Miguel, many people volunteered information about the location of private chapels that I could never have ferreted out myself. In the end, I located, and photographed, nearly 300 churches and chapels, about one-fourth of which are abandoned and/or privately held. Still, the count almost certainly falls short of the actual number. Most of the new chapels remain unfinished and are comparatively uninteresting. It must also be borne in mind that the number of chapels that actually exist is subject to interpretation because a church may contain several chapels. The Atotonilco complex, for example, contains six separate chapels, and several of the churches in San Miguel have two or three capillas within their walls.

The Greek word "ecclesia," which came to mean "church" was originally applied to an official assembly of citizens. In Spanish, of course, the word remains almost identical—"iglesia." The word "chapel," *capilla* in Spanish, has a very different etymology. It is derived from the Latin "capella," the diminutive of *cappa*, or cloak, the name given to the shrine in which the cloak of St. Martin was kept and carried about by the Frankish kings on their journeys and military campaigns. Eventually it came to apply to any sanctuary containing relics. The word was finally identified with all places of worship that were not mother churches. In Mexico, as in the United States, "chapel" is usually meant to express the idea of a small church. A religious building, in Spanish, may be referred to as "parroquia," "iglesia," "oratorio," "capilla," "templo," "convento," "calvario," "monasterio," or "santuario."

The photographs in the book are arranged in a geographic fashion, that is, the first photographs are of churches in the center of San Miguel, beginning, of course, with La Parroquia. Then, as the sequence begins, the churches and chapels that are to be found farther from the center are shown, and so on. The last church pictured is in Puerto de Nieto, a dozen miles from La Parroquia.

I have not concentrated on the interiors of the churches. The abandoned chapels, of course, have no trace left of interior furnishings. The new chapels have particularly plain interiors and a disheartening sameness. Even the older chapels still in use seldom retain the beautiful furnishings and decorations they once had. Plastic flowers and decorations dominate.

This was not always true. A book called *Mexican Churches* by the photographers Ellen Auerbach and Eliot Porter with pictures, mostly of interiors, made in the 1950s, offers superb examples of the delicate and delightful decorations then still much in evidence. For example, a number of the photographs were made inside the chapel of Tirado, a few miles outside of San Miguel. Today, only crumpled walls remain of that hacienda, and nothing of the chapel.

I have tried to show the unknown, the unfinished and the vernacular, along with the spectacular. I made the photographs using 35mm Olympus cameras with lenses ranging from 24mm to 300mm. Although I abhor using telephoto lenses, the 300mm lens allowed me to photograph details of church towers that otherwise would have been impossible. I used Fujichrome 100 Professional transparency film. I consciously chose to make most of the photographs during the winter and spring, with its reliable weather. After the rains start, usually beginning in June, many of the roads become impassable, and the sun sometimes doesn't show for days. On the other hand, during those months the desert miraculously turns into a garden, the land is green, and there are fields of flowers everywhere, presenting an entirely new landscape in which the chapels also appear differently.

Finding the churches and chapels of San Miguel de Allende proved to be a wonderful adventure, and photographing them an unusually satisfying experience. The Appendix lists the churches I've been able to find and supplies some (necessarily vague) directions. Anyone interested in visiting these treasures could contact local guides or taxi drivers. The small map on the last page might also provide a start.

Or venture out on your own. There are still more chapels out there somewhere, undiscovered, yet to be photographed and enjoyed. And don't forget the lollipops for the children.

INTRODUCTION

Many of the churches of Mexico are architectural gems ... that compare favorably with the noted cathedrals of Europe, and he who forgets this over-looks one of the most important factors in Mexican history and civilization.

- George Wharton James
The Old Missions of California

There are more than 30,000 churches in Mexico, about 1,000 in Mexico City alone, the world's largest city. There are almost 300 churches in and around San Miguel de Allende, a small munic-ipality near the geographic center of Mexico and, some say, its pretti-est. More than three dozen churches and chapels are tucked away in the federally protected "Historic District" of San Miguel, while the rest are spread throughout the surrounding campo—the country-side—of the less than 600 square miles of the municipio, an area only about half the size of Rhode Island (America's smallest state). That amounts to one-tenth of one percent of the size of Mexico, yet San Miguel de Allende acccounts for about one percent of all the religious structures in all of Mexico—ten times the average. Why? There are several reasons: one is the fact of geography, the other the fancy of his-tory.

Geography is destiny. The tale is told that when the king of Spain asked one of the conquistadores what New Spain looked like, the soldier picked up a piece of paper, crumpled it, then placed it on the table. "Like this, Your Majesty," was the reply. Mostly mountain-ous, only one-tenth of Mexico is suitable for agriculture. But the municipio of San Miguel lies on the edge of the Bajío, Mexico's bread basket. Although hardly flat (perhaps less than one-third of the land is suitable for crops), much of the rest lends itself to the raising of livestock. About 125,000 people live in the district, nearly half in or near the town, the rest spread throughout more than 200 separate hamlets. Some of these little pueblitos may have only a few dozen inhabitants, others as many as 500. Still, every village has its church or chapel.

The Río Laja, running north to south, the only significant stream, neatly divides the municipality in half. It was on its banks that the territory was first settled. (In 1967, as a flood control measure, the Presa Ignacio Allende, a huge reservoir nearly 8 miles long, was created west of the town of San Miguel.)

All the terrain of the municipio lies above 6,000 feet, with some peaks of Los Picachos, the mountain range southeast of the town, reaching nearly 9,000 feet. Much of the area west of the river is rugged, with deep ravines (and two of the oldest *templos* in the area — the pyramids of La Cañada de la Virgen). The northeastern quadrant is considerably flatter, but remained sparsely settled until the second half of the 20th century when irrigation, made possible with electrically operated pumps, allowed for productive vegetable farming. Dozens of tiny communities sprang up for the farm workers and their families.

In the last five centuries much of the landscape has changed. Deforestation and over-grazing and the subsequent erosion of the soil has done much to damage a fragile, semi-desert ecosystem, and forced a redistribution of much of the population. Villages have disappeared and churches abandoned because many campesinos, unable to feed themselves, moved to the cities to look for jobs. (As in most countries, more than half of Mexico's population now lives in cities.)

Hernán Cortés landed near Veracruz on Good Friday in 1519 with 550 men, 16 horses, 14 cannons, and a handful of dogs, and in little more than two years the Aztec empire was defeated. The incredible story of the Conquest is well-known, but it is sometimes forgotten that Diego Velasquez, the governor of Cuba, instructed Cortés to

"Bear in mind from the beginning that the first aim of your expedition is to serve God and spread the Christian Faith."

Immediately after the Conquest of Mexico the evangelization began. The first three Franciscan friars, from Belgium, arrived in 1523. But in conscious imitation of the Twelve Apostles, twelve Franciscans were dispatched to Mexico in 1524, and became the most successful of the first wave of missionaries. Dominicans and Augustinians soon followed. While the sword won lands for the Spanish Crown, the cross won souls and consolidated the empire. The Spanish Conquest was the joint enterprise of adventure-seeking soldiers and earnest friars. (In 1537, by a specific Bull from Rome, Indians were declared to be human beings with souls, susceptible to conversion.)

About two decades after the Conquest a Franciscan friar named Juan de San Miguel founded a tiny settlement on the banks of the Río Laja and named it San Miguel de las Chichimecas after his patron saint and the dominant (and hostile) Indian tribe of the region. Scholars quibble about a year here or there; the official estimate is 1542, although it was likely a few years earlier.

The original settlement, near what is now called San Miguel Viejo, a small rancho a mile or so beyond the outskirts of town, boasted a small chapel, no doubt made of rocks, tree limbs, and branches. The village was soon abandoned. The river proved to be both an unreliable source of water in the winter, and prone to flooding in the summer. Some historians speculate that mosquitos, and attendant diseases, may have been a serious problem. Much of Mexico's population was decimated by European diseases within the first few decades after the Conquest.

In any case, legend has it that a thirsty dog discovered a spring (now called El Chorro—the Spurt) at the foot of a hill a few miles to the east. The settlement was moved near the spring, a small chapel built (nothing remains of the original), and San Miguel found its home. The new location was also more readily defendable, of great importance during the first half century after the Conquest.

It was, and remains, a splendid site. At an altitude of 6,300 feet, San Miguel offers a nearly flawless climate, cool in the summer, spring-like in winter. The views from the hillside are incomparable, with the Guanajuato Mountains looming in the west, the countryside visible from the center of town.

When silver was discovered later in the 16th century, first in Zacatecas, then in San Luis Potosí and Guanajuato, San Miguel's humble evangelical raison d'être was changed: it became a garrison town to help guard the silver shipments on their way to Mexico City, thence to Veracruz, and ultimately to Spain.

In 1555 the Viceroy Don Luis de Velasco mandated that "in order to avoid the killings and robberies which the Chichimecs have carried out on the road to Zacatecas, let there be founded at the village of San Miguel a Spanish City for the security of that road." The mandate allowed for a presidio, a fort, to be built. Once the city was founded, its ecclesiastical position was also defined and a parish church established in 1564. And for a time San Miguel ended up with six patron saints: John the Baptist, Our Lady of Guadalupe, Our Lady of Loreto, the Immaculate Conception, St. Joseph, and, of course, St. Michael. (There was an attempt by the civil government in 1789 to suppress some of the festivities surrounding those saint days, but the people defended the festivals and funmaking with every measure, and even today San Miguel is famed for the number of its fiestas.)

From the wealth generated, and for its growing size, the town soon earned the name of San Miguel el Grande, to distinguish it from the many San Miguels that had sprouted in Mexico. As the town grew, many small agricultural communities were established along the banks of the Río Laja to support the growing population.

The riches of the town of San Miguel were displayed by the erection of a great number of churches and other religious structures, such as monasteries and convents. The 18th century saw an astonishing amount of building and re-building, much of it still preserved.

San Miguel, of course, was the cradle of the struggle for independence with Spain. Captain Ignacio Allende, born in San Miguel el Grande, was one of its leaders at the beginning of the rebellion in 1810. In 1826, five years after the Republic of Mexico was founded, the town was renamed after its great hero.

San Miguel de Allende remained a quiet town for much of the next century, but in the late 1930s an American artist and writer named Stirling Dickinson arrived, and it hasn't been the same since. Dickinson encouraged other artists and intellectuals to move to San Miguel, and after World War II, several art schools were founded, among them the Instituto Allende, for years headed by Dickinson. In the ensuing years San Miguel became a Mecca for writers and artists, many of them expatriate Americans, Canadians, and Europeans. It is thought that today there are around 3,000 full-time foreign residents.

San Miguel de Allende's architecture, ecclesiastical and civil, continues to be admired and revered by both Mexicans and expatriates. (In 1926 the town was declared a national historic monument.) But much of its vernacular architecture in the countryside has escaped notice because of the difficulty of travel.

Catholic liturgy and ritual dazzled the Indians; ceremony filled a visual, and perhaps an emotional, need. Chapels were built in each community. However, the aboriginal population managed to dilute, mix, and disguise traces of its own rich religious heritage and to graft this onto the context, strength and splendor of Catholicism. The same applied to its architecture.

Evangelization created a need for churches, convents, and schools, and the building of towns and villages was encouraged, since a dispersed population made the work of the Church more difficult.

The construction of the various religious buildings in Mexico accomplished by the friars in the 16th century has few parallels in history. In less than half a century the landscape of much of Mexico was changed profoundly. As the historian Donna Pierce has written:

"They began by baptizing Indians by the thousands, replacing pagan deities with Christian images and assuming the position of religious leadership vacated by the native priests. Small temporary chapels were rapidly constructed and the open chapel, one of the architectural solutions unique to the New World, was invented. This structure, an open-sided chancel or chapel, was built to house the altar, the Host, and the celebrating priests, while the congregation stood in the churchyard that functioned as an outdoor nave. In some cases . . . the open chapel was eventually incorporated into the church structure; in others . . . the open nave was roofed but not walled; in still others, the open chapel and atrium continued to function alongside the completed church. This building type evolved in response to several conditions: the Mexican Indians were accustomed to outdoor religious services; an immense number of Indian converts had to be accommodated in the early period; and large churches could not be constructed rapidly."

The many primitive Indian chapels in the campo around San Miguel display curious representations of saints, crosses, and other religious themes. The building of these chapels, known as the "Calvarios de la Conquista," was authorized by royal decree after requests from prominent Indian chiefs and from the Spanish conquerors. Spain was only too eager to accede. In return for these concessions the Spanish Crown obtained the political (and religious) loyalty of the people. And in the small chapels the Indian would be free to worship in his own way his own sacred images. The friars often permitted the Indians to add pre-Hispanic decorations and symbols to the façades. Sometimes these façades display a curious mixture of Baroque and pre-Christian elements.

The 17th century brought the gradual emergence of the Baroque style, but San Miguel was too far away from the main population centers to participate that early. Nothing in that style was built in San Miguel in that century. However, the 18th century proved to be most significant for San Miguel.

That century brought High Baroque to San Miguel. Its most exuberant form is the Churrigueresque, named after José Benito Churriguera (1665-1725), a Spanish architect whose lively style found its way into many Mexican architectural treasures. His style was unrestrained with boundless ornamentation. The column, still clearly recognizable as such in the Baroque style, is broken up into such a variety of forms and so much altered in character that the original form is sometimes completely lost. The main distinguishing characteristic of the style is the pilaster (estípite) in the form of a truncated pyramid standing on its smaller end, a feature frequently found on church façades and, within the church, on altar screens.

Toward the end of the 18th century the neoclassical style made its debut. It was welcomed as a way to help Mexico break away from the powerful Spanish heritage. During the hundred years between the War of Independence and the Revolution no significant developments occurred in Mexican architecture. The most recent architecture of the chapels in San Miguel can only be described as workmanlike, but uninspired.

Many of the churches within the city of San Miguel, described below, are well-known and indeed extraordinary. But a far greater number in the campo around the city evokes the same response: these vernacular structures show the same craftsmanship, the same devotion, and the same discipline as the better-known (and larger) churches in the town.

Most chapels and churches have a large forecourt, or atrium, sometimes with a stone or wooden cross in the center. Entrances are almost always arched. The buildings display interesting representations of saints, crosses, and other religious themes. There is almost always a calvario, a small doorless niche within which stand crosses and flowers, and where candles are usually displayed. The calvario is a shrine dedicated to the souls of the departed. Here the souls receive homage and prayer. The Indian, on fulfilling a religious vow, does not enter the chapel immediately. He stops and kneels at the small calvario. There he prays, makes offerings, and burns incense. With contrition, he asks permission of the outer cross and of the blessed souls before he enters the chapel.

Though the Indians adopted the Gospel, they did not completely give up their ancient rites. Religions do not disappear overnight; they die slowly and gradually. And at the end only faint traces of older patterns remain.

The primitive and animistic cult of the Indians of this area was understood by the Spaniards. The Indians followed a process which has been visible among the other native groups on the American continent, and continued to worship souls and natural phenomena such as the sun, the moon, the rainbow, the stars and the wind. The Indian allies of the Spanish conquerors realized that it would not be wise for the government to erase the ancient myths and popular beliefs.

By the early 19th century the Church held one half of all the real estate and capital of Mexico. Most of the clergy had been opposed to the independence movement, and it comes as no surprise that shortly after Mexico gained its independence from Spain, anti-Catholic legislation started to appear. While President Benito Juárez was in office during the late 1860s more laws were passed calling for the abolition of the privileges of the Church.

The 1917 Constitution contains a dizzying number of anti-religious provisions which apply to all religions but were designed for, and principally apply, to the Catholic Church. For example, marriages in the church are not recognized, since legal status is denied to all religions. (Still, nearly 70 percent of couples are also married in church.) Churches and other religious buildings, and lands, are considered state property. People may use the churches, but government approval is required before additions or alteration can be made.

Religious schools are not allowed. Members of the clergy (both nuns and priests) may not vote or discuss politics, and until recently were not allowed to wear clerical garb in public. Priests must be Mexican-born, and their numbers are strictly regulated.

These provisions were mostly honored in the breach until the presidency of Plutarco Elías Calles (1924-1928), who in autocratic fashion pursued the constitutional reforms. This conflict with the church led to the bloody Cristero wars (1926-1929). No mass was allowed to be celebrated, at least legally, anywhere in Mexico for several years. The Vatican broke off relations with Mexico. (It wasn't until 1992 that constitutional reforms paved the way for the re-opening of diplomatic relations with the Vatican.) The Church has lost much of its political power. Although it is claimed that over 90 percent of all Mexicans are baptized into the faith, this nominal Catholicism is less and less actively practiced. Still, churches and chapels continue to be built wherever new communities are created, and in most of the older ranchos chapels continue to be used, and sometimes even enlarged.

Catholicism in Mexico has been described as "a Baroque Christianity heavily influenced by pagan traditions." This remains true and clearly evident in the rich architectural heritage of the churches of San Miguel de Allende. Almost one-half date back to the 18th and 19th centuries. The formal and vernacular religious architecture of San Miguel is a reflection of the landscape, the environment, the climate and the spirit of its inhabitants. Of course the Catholic church left strong impressions upon the architecture. The churches of San Miguel continue to proclaim both the splendor of bygone years and the continuing intense fervor of this community.

Wrote the great historian Henry Bamford Parkes in *A History of Mexico:* "The churches were the one valuable legacy bequeathed by colonial Catholicism to modern Mexico—the only lasting monument of that prodigious faith which had inspired the noblest of the Spanish empire-builders."

The following are brief descriptions of some of the churches and chapels in and around San Miguel de Allende:

La Parroquia de San Miguel Arcángel

It is always called just that: La Parroquia, the parish church. It is San Miguel's best-known icon, featured on innumerable posters and post-cards, the subject of every tourist's snapshots, the background for every vacationing family's video.

It is not a cathedral, as some think. Much of the building is not even very old, the pink-spired façade only being finished in the 1880s, a veneer over a structure that was begun at the end of the 17th century by an architect named Marco Antonio Sobrarias on the site of a still older edifice. A photograph of the church made in the 1870s shows a handsome, although conventional building with twin towers, one slightly higher than the other. Zeferino Gutiérrez changed all that.

Gutiérrez, a native of San Miguel, was a self-taught Indian architect and builder, who, it is said, received his inspiration and notions about ecclesiastical architecture from postcards of the great cathedrals in Europe. He convinced the religious authorities of the excellence of his pseudo-Gothic design and on October 8, 1880 work was started on the new façade of La Parroquia. The story is often told, usually derisively, that the master-builder scratched and sketched his plans in the dirt so that his illiterate workmen could understand his intentions. But the tale rings true: after all, the illiterate craftsmen who built great structures elsewhere in the world received their information in much the same way.

The result is a mass of pink pilasters, balustrades, windows, spires and steeples that soars over the grand houses that rim the Jardín. It continues to invite invective from architectural critics. Francisco de la Maza, for example, in his history of San Miguel, called it "an architectonic error . . . abominable." Others have pejoratively referred to it as "grotesque gothesque," and "Disneyesque." But as

Robert Somerlott has written, "The common people of the town love it, boast of it, recall it with longing when they are away. That, perhaps, was the builder's finest achievement."

Much of the Sobrarias building remained intact behind the new façade. As late as the 1940s two new chapels were built within. The interior is a curious mishmash of the good, the bad, and the ugly. The camarín, the space in which ceremonial vestments for the different images of saints are kept, was constructed by the great Mexican architect Francisco Eduardo Tresguerras (1765-1833), who added another dome above the camarín, and a burial vault underneath. Hundreds are buried there, among them twice-President Anastasio Bustamante, who spent his last years in San Miguel, and several heros of the War of Independence. (The Emperor Maximilian inspected the crypt during a visit to San Miguel, remarked on its beauty, and pronounced it "worthy of a king." Shortly afterward, in 1867, he was executed in Querétaro, but it was not his fate to be buried in San Miguel.) The vault is reached through a small stairwell to the right of the altar. It is open to the public on November 2, the Day of the Dead.

The baptistery font in the first chapel to the left is remarkably beautiful, while some of the murals in other side chapels are startlingly ugly.

There is a much-revered treasure in La Parroquia. In the second side chapel on the left side of the church is an ancient 16th century statue of El Señor de la Conquista, The Lord of the Conquest, an image made by Indians from Pátzcuaro from the heart of cornstalks mixed with the mucilage of orchid bulbs. It figures large in the fiesta of the same name, held on the first Friday in March, when Indian *concheros* celebrate with continuous dancing in the atrium of La Parroquia.

St. Michael's Day falls on September 29, but is celebrated on the weekend nearest that date. Since St. Michael is the city's patron saint, this fiesta is perhaps the most notable of the dozens that occur throughout the year, and all its related activities take place in front of La Parroquia.

There are eight bells in the tower of La Parroquia. They all have names. The largest, called La Luz, was cast in 1732 and still calls the faithful to prayer. It is said that certain noble families donated gold which was melted with the bronze "in order to heighten the sound of the bell and make it clearer." It must have worked, for the tone of La Luz blends nicely with the others in the tower that each have names like San Pedro and San Miguel.

There always seems to be something going on in La Parroquia: daily masses, weddings, baptisms, even concerts on occasion. A private tour is easily arranged with the mayordomo, who can be contacted through the parish office to the left of the church.

La Iglesia de San Rafael or *La Santa Escuela de Cristo*

La Parroquia so dominates the south side of the Jardín that the smaller church to the left is often thought to be part of it. To be sure, they share the same atrium, but there the similarity ends. Unlike La Parroquia, San Rafael faces west. It competes with the Tercera Orden church (see page 22) for the honor of being the oldest church. Its construction was begun shortly after 1564, when the parish was authorized by the bishop of Michoacán, the illustrious Vasco de Quiroga. And so it was the original parish church. It has two names: San Rafael (also an archangel, like San Miguel) is favored by scholars, while Santa Escuela de Cristo is the popular name used by the people. The latter name is derived from a pious association known as the "Holy School of Christ," founded in the church in 1742 by Father Luis Felipe Neri de Alfaro, the most influential cleric in the history of San Miguel, sponsor of the church of La Salud, and the builder and patron of the Sanctuary of Atotonilco.

Like its neighbor, Santa Escuela, too, lost its original tower to remodeling and received a new north-facing façade, designed by

Zeverino Gutiérrez and also executed in the neo-Gothic style of La Parroquia. The western façade of the church itself was not changed, and remains as the severe original with its small sculpture of Christ, and a tiny medallion.

The statue on top of the pillar in front of the church is of Diez de Sollano, a native of San Miguel who became the first bishop of León when this part of Mexico became a separate diocese. He was the first Mexican-born cleric to reach that high office.

In 1762 a clock was installed in the original tower of the church. (Soon after, Calle Reloj—Clock Street—received its name.) The clock was a gift to San Miguel el Grande from the city of Madrid. When the new tower was built around the turn of the century (and a new clock installed) the original was moved to the tower of the newly-built waterworks at El Chorro.

The church is dark and gloomy, but there is a small side chapel that is bright and cheerful, even if the images of the suffering Christ tend to be seriously depressing. The funds for its construction were contributed by Zeferino Gutiérrez.

The clock is the town's official time-keeper, and its bells toll every quarter-hour. The method of telling time by the sound is a mystery to most people, but it is really quite easy: two different tones are sounded. At first there are two peals: one set of two strikes at a quarter after; two sets of two on the half hour; three sets of two at a quarter to the hour; and four sets of two on the hour. Then, after a short interval a different sounding bell tolls the hour. For example, half past four sounds like "ding-ding, ding-ding; dong, dong, dong, dong."

There are nearly a hundred bells hanging from the various *campanarios* and *espadañas* in San Miguel. Some citizens suspect there are many more; the cacophony can be ear-splitting and nerve-wracking. Feast days of saints and national holidays especially are singled out for serenades, but there are times when even the oldest citizens of San Miguel roll their eyes when asked what the occasion might be.

El Templo de la Tercera Orden

On the pleasant little park on Calle San Francisco, one block east of the Jardín, is located the church of the Third Order. It is one of the two oldest churches in San Miguel, competing with (portions) of San Rafael for that title. It is known that the monastery behind the church is older, perhaps as much as a century, but the church was officially consecrated in 1713, although possibly finished somewhat earlier. Small, simple and austere, even sporting a huge flying buttress on its southern side, it stands in sharp contrast to the incredible ornateness of the façade of its neighbor, the San Francisco church. A statue of St. Francis stands in a niche above the front door, which displays several carved wooden panels with the symbols of the Franciscan Order, the crossed arms of God, bare and white, and a Franciscan, robed and brown. Three stone plaques flanking the door show crosses with tongues of fire emanating, a reference to the Pentecost when the apostles received the gift of speaking in tongues, reminding us that this was a missionary church. On the side façade is a vaulted niche with a statue of San Diego, the patron saint of Spain, while above it a huge carved cross of Lorraine (with its twin crosspieces) is displayed.

This modest church is crowned by a slender and handsome angular steeple. It was probably added later in the middle of the 18th century. The interior is as stark as the outside, and sparsely decorated with small depictions of the fourteen authorized Stations of the Cross, a few statues of saints, and a huge mural showing sinners being saved from the fires of hell.

La Iglesia de San Francisco

The church of San Francisco was built during the last two decades of the 18th century, and represents two completely different architectural philosophies. The elaborate Baroque façade stands in great contrast with the stark base of the tower. (One bewildered tourist was overheard saying, "Why would they have used concrete blocks ?")

It is still sometimes referred to as the "Spanish church," to distinguish it from the "Indian church," (see Oratorio, page 25).The first stone of the church was laid on June 29, 1779. Funds for its construction were raised from wealthy families in town, and even by fund-raising events such as bullfights.

There are two façades, but it is the south-facing side that has inspired comments ranging from "wonderful" to "mad" to "insane" to "magnificent." It is all of those. It is lavishly ornamented in the Churrigueresque style. José Churriguera's style nearly outwitted the Baroque, and this façade contains some of the finest, graceful estípites (pilasters in the shape of truncated, inverted obelisks) and a collection of famous saints of the Franciscan Order, flowers, cherubs, vines and virgins. A statue of St. Francis crowns the façade and looks down on it all, while the image of the crucified Christ is displayed somewhat lower, above a stained-glass window, and flanked by representations of Our Lady of Sorrows and of St. John. The dome of the church is covered with blue and white tiles.

But while construction was proceeding during the last decade of the 18th century, the winds of change were blowing. The church authorities in Mexico became concerned about the jubilant, exuberant and "excessive" aspects of the Baroque style. The neoclassic style had arrived in Mexico before the bell tower had even been built, and this accounts for the plainness of the tower and walls adjoining the face of the church.

The bell tower, as well as the dome and the interior, thought to be designed by the architect Eduardo Tresguerras, the leading architect of the region, were finished at the end of the second decade of its construction, on April 13, 1799.

The interior of the church is quite beautiful and spacious, but as different from the glorious exterior as the central façade is different from its flanking walls.

A small tile on the side of the entrance says "Convento de San

Antonio," confusing many visitors. It refers to the old convent behind both Tercera Orden and San Francisco, still occupied by friars of the Franciscan order.

The feastday of San Francisco is celebrated on October 8.

El Templo de Nuestra Señora de la Salud

The Temple of Our Lady of Health, another fine example of early Churrigueresque decoration, is located in the middle of an astonishing complex of religious buildings, several blocks long, that face the Plaza Cívica with its statue of General Ignacio Allende on his horse. The building is surmounted with an enormous scallop shell, a motif common to neoclassicism, and seen often in San Miguel architecture. It is thought to be related to a baptism performed by San Diego, who used a sea shell as a container. Over the Moorish-influenced front door are sculptures of the Immaculate Conception flanked by St. Joachim and St. Ann. Flanking the door itself are statues of the Sacred Heart and St. John the Evangelist.

The dome of the church is composed of multi-hued tiles while the pink lantern of the dome has suggested to many people the form of the prickly pear, the fruit of the nopal cactus.

The church was finished in 1735, built using monies donated by Father Luis Felipe Neri de Alfaro, who years later built Atotonilco. It originally served as the chapel for the College of San Francisco de Sales which adjoins the church. The church inside is small and charming. The chapel on the right is dedicated to the Virgen de la Salud. On the left there is an icon of the Holy Child of Health, surrounded by many snapshots, toys and articles of clothing of children whose health was miraculously recovered. At the top of the corner dome supports are paintings of four females representing Prudence, Temperance, Fortitude, and Justice. On November 22, the Day of St. Cecilia, the patroness of musicians and the blind, musicians come to the church to serenade the Virgin.

El Oratorio de San Felipe Neri

Situated at the western-most portion of the complex of religious buildings facing the Plaza Cívica, the Oratorio replaced, in 1712, an older chapel, called Ecce Homo, that belonged to the Confraternity of Mulattos. It was built at the urging of Don Juan Antonio Pérez de Espinosa, a priest from Pátzcuaro, who had been asked to deliver several sermons in San Miguel, and who had, as many have since, fallen in love with the town. He received permission to move permanently and founded the local community of the Order of San Felipe Neri. For reasons that remain unclear, the priest and many of the prominent residents of the town wanted to build a new church on the site of Ecce Homo. The Indians, having built the chapel with their own funds and labor, demurred, but subsequent legal battles cleared the way for Espinosa to proceed and the Indians acquiesced.

The original entrance of Ecce Homo was retained on the east side of the new building and can be seen by entering the small courtyard to the right of the church. A cross of Lorraine and a small sculpture of "La Virgen de la Soledad" can be seen above this portal.

Many changes and adaptations were made, and the church was finished in 1714. Eventually the name Ecce Homo was forgotten and the new church was called El Oratorio de San Felipe Neri. It is the most popular church in town. The façade of the church is a beautiful example of Baroque architecture and superb workmanship.

The five statues in the niches represent St. Joseph, St. John the Baptist, St. Philip, St. Peter and St. Paul. A number of paintings chronicling the life of San Felipe Neri may be found inside. Perhaps the most notable aspect of the church is the Chapel of la Santa Casa de Loreto, located in its left transept (see next description).

La Santa Casa de Loreto

The chapel within the Oratorio is a replica of the famous Holy House in Loreto, Italy, which is, according to an "authorized" legend of the

Roman Catholic Church (that is, one is urged, but not required, to believe it) the actual house of the Virgin Mary in Nazareth. When the Infidels captured the Holy Land, this house fell into their hands. As the story goes, this so infuriated the angels that, under the command of St. Michael, they transported the entire house, lock, stock and barrel to Loreto, Italy, where it may still be seen, as can be done in San Miguel by visiting the left transept of El Oratorio.

Since the Virgin of Loreto was the patroness of the wealthy Canal family, Don Manuel Tomás de la Canal y Bueno de Baeza (the name is also commemorated in San Miguel as Calle Canal and Calle Baeza) founded and constructed the Santa Casa in 1735. It cost 35,000 pesos, an unimaginable sum of money in those days, but reflecting the wealth that was available during the "Golden Age" of San Miguel el Grande.

An inscription in the archway to the entrance says, "This is the home in which the Son of God was conceived." The floor and lower walls are covered with glazed tiles from China, Spain, and Puebla, Mexico. Other parts of the walls are covered with finely woven and patterned gold cloth. The octagonal *camarín* behind has six altars. The donors, Don Manuel and his wife Doña María de Hervas de Flores, are depicted in stone niches on either side of the room. They are buried under the floor of the first room, often referred to as the Living Room.

The second room is the Bedroom. The walls of this octagonal space are covered with gold leaf. This is the most sumptuous religious building in San Miguel, and another outstanding example of the exuberant Baroque style that flourished during the 18th century.

La Iglesia de Santa Ana

The squat and solid Iglesia de Santa Ana one block west of the Oratorio dominates part of a block of Calle Insurgentes which was also once called Santa Ana. At the end of the 18th century a member of the San Felipe Neri Order founded a home on this site for "pious" (read impoverished, probably widowed) women and later a small orphanage. The original church has been substituted by the present one, built in 1847. The grounds of the Biblioteca Pública next door were once part of this extensive complex, which at one time also included a nunnery. The church has no bell tower, but on the west side there is a small *espadaña* from which three bells are suspended.

La Iglesia y Convento de la Concepción

The Church and Convent of La Concepción on Calle Canal one block west of the Jardín, and better known as Las Monjas — The Nuns — is an architectural treasure made possible by María Josefa Lina de la Canal y Hervas, the eldest daughter of Manuel Tomás de la Canal who donated the monies to build Santa Casa de Loreto.

María Josefa used her considerable inheritance to build this edifice, although some other San Miguel residents contributed. The royal decree to proceed was signed by Ferdinand VI in September 1754; construction was begun the following year on a plot of land then known as The House of Orange Trees. The building was still incomplete eleven years later when the nuns of the Immaculate Conception moved in. There was no dome, presbytery, tower, or even an altar. The bell tower was not finished until 1842.

The dome was finally finished in 1891, ornamented with pairs of Corinthian columns on the lower level and with a balustrade and statues of saints on the upper level. It is thought that the architect of the dome of the church, Zeferino Gutiérrez, was inspired by the Church of Les Invalides in Paris.

The church is somber and austere, but with many admirable details: the gilded altar piece in the lower choir, polychrome sculptures of St. Joseph and the Immaculate Conception, and a number of interesting paintings, including several by Miguel Antonio Martínez de Pocasangre, the creator of the frescoes at Atotonilco (see page 30).

The monumental two-story neoclassical cloister that adjoins the church, formerly the residence of the nuns, is now part of the National Institute of Fine Arts. Officially called Centro Cultural Ignacio Ramírez "El Nigromante" (The Sorcerer), it is popularly known as Bellas Artes.

La Iglesia de Santo Domingo

Santo Domingo, at the top of Calle Correo, was built at the end of the 18th century. Once part of a home for pious and impoverished women, Dominican nuns now run a primary school here. Although it looks, when viewed from below, as if there are four bells, there are, in fact, five—a small *espadaña* to the side houses a fifth.

La Capilla del Calvario

At the beginning of the Salida Real a Querétaro at the top of Calle San Francisco stands a tiny chapel called El Calvario—Calvary—the perfect name for a little church on the top of a hill. The Via Dolorosa—The Way of the Cross—with its Fourteen Stations, appropriately enough ends here. The Way of the Cross procession takes place on Wednesday during Easter Week.

La Ermita de Nuestra Señora de Loreto

La Ermita (The Hermitage) is a small shrine on the road that used to be called El Camino Real—The Royal Road—then became known as Calle Pedro Vargas, after the famous Mexican troubadour, who owned a house not far away on the same street, but is now mostly referred to as the Salida a Querétaro, the Exit to Querétaro. The hotel next door was built by the Mexican comedian and actor Cantinflas. Both the chapel and the alley that border it to the north are sometimes called Loreto because when the image of the Virgin of the Santa Casa chapel in the Oratorio was brought from Europe it was stored for some time in this building. A member of the Order of San Felipe Neri,

Father Luis Caballero de Acuña, supervised the reconstruction of the chapel in 1736; its previous history is unknown.

La Parroquia de San Antonio

A short distance west of the Instituto Allende stands the parish church of San Antonio. It is a popular church: St. Anthony is associated with marriage, and on Tuesdays the faithful will beg San Antonio for the grace of matrimony. The church remained a rather simple edifice, without a dome, until the 1960s. To evade the laws against the expansion of churches, that dome, and other finishing touches made to the church, was decades in the making, much of it accomplished on the sly. It is the starting point for the bizarre Fiesta de los Locos, held on the weekend nearest June 13, St. Anthony's feast day.

El Templo de San Juan de Dios

A few blocks northwest of the Jardín there is a church—and a neighborhood—called San Juan de Dios. The church was established in 1770, and some years later a hospital was built next door. The hospital, no longer in use, has become a school. The pleasant and pretty courtyard has been kept much as it was two centuries ago.

This is where for a short period preceding Easter Week the much venerated statue of Our Lord of the Column, usually kept in Atotonilco, is displayed after a night-long procession from there.

Other Chapels Around the Town of San Miguel

Every barrio, colonia, fraccionamiento—every neighborhood, subdivision, and development—has its chapel.

Older neighborhoods around San Miguel have interesting and charming chapels. There is San José, near the top of the Cuesta de San José on the way to Los Balcones; along the Salida a Querétaro there are several, some secreted behind the walls of private residences.

Some chapels, like Valle del Maíz, near the eastern end of the

Salida a Querétaro, maintain a high community profile and an active fiesta schedule. A poor neighborhood called Las Cuevitas, near the bus station, has two within a block of each other. The chapels of Ojo de Agua and La Palmita are devilishly difficult to find, but well worth the effort, as are the abandoned, and ruined, chapels at Atascadero and on Calle Piedras Chinas.

The rapid population growth in the last 20 years has produced a number of suburbs around the historic district. Nearly all of these new neighborhoods have chapels, most of them under construction. All are listed in the Appendix.

Chapels Around the Countryside

It is fortunate that one of the most interesting and beautiful of the chapels in the countryside surrounding San Miguel should be San Miguel Viejo, located only about a mile west of the railroad station, near the site of the original settlement of San Miguel. It is not, of course, the original chapel built by Fray Juan de San Miguel. Most scholars agree that is was built between 1720 and 1730.

Beyond San Miguel Viejo, none of the more than 200 chapels in the campo of the municipality of San Miguel de Allende are within walking distance, yet none are further than about a dozen miles from the center of town.

All the structures beyond the city of San Miguel are tiny, with the exception of Atotonilco (see below) and the *parroquias* at Cruz del Palmar, Los Rodríguez, Puerto de Nieto, and Jalpa. Except for the (contemporary) chapel at the Benedictine retreat near Atotonilco, all were designed and built by anonymous, indigenous workers.

El Santuario de Atotonilco

About eight miles north of San Miguel, a mile or so off the road to Dolores Hidalgo, is the shrine of Atotonilco. Atotonilco in Nahuatl means "place of hot waters," (there are a number of thermal springs nearby) and an ascetic priest from San Miguel who had some years earlier sponsored the building of the Templo de la Salud there, was concerned: "This spot has been a place of lawlessness and sensuality," he wrote. "Under the pretext of healthful bathing there have been contests, music, feasts, games, and other sins."

And so in 1740 Father Luis Felipe Neri de Alfaro founded the shrine of Atotonilco, dedicated to penitence. Construction was mostly finished by 1748, although several chapels and many other buildings were added later. It has become a famous pilgrimage center and one of the great shrines of Mexico.

Passing this way on September 16, 1810, Father Miguel Hidalgo, from the town of Dolores, 18 miles north, where he had the previous evening proclaimed Mexican independence, stopped here with his rag-tag army and took the image of the Virgin of Guadalupe from the church and fastened it to his banner, thus making her the patroness of the Mexican liberation movement.

In 1802 then-lieutenant José Ignacio María de Allende y Unzaga was married here, thus associating Atotonilco forever with two of the great heroes of the War of Independence.

The church and the various chapels within have fine frescoes of folk themes covering walls, ceilings, and domes, mostly by Miguel Antonio Martínez de Pocasangre. Pocasangre also incorporated poetry and sermons by Father Alfaro on the walls. The sanctuary is dedicated to Jesus the Nazarene, whose life-size image occupies the place above the High Altar in the old church. It contains six small chapels: Belén, Loreto, Soledad, Nuestra Señora del Rosario, La Purísima, and El Calvario or Santo Sepulcro. In the *camarín* behind the High Altar are statues of the Virgin and the Apostles.

To quote from the *Official Guide to San Miguel Allende:* "The interior of the shrine of Atotonilco, together with its chapels, vaults, domes and dome lanterns, is covered with fresco paintings. The walls are alive with a multitude of divine and human personages, angels, archangels and devils, leaves, flowers and fruits, inscriptions, sonnets and poems of a mystical nature. The burst of color and imagination brings to life the inexhaustible fantasy of the men who planned this great artistic adventure. In the church of Atotonilco one is exposed to a significant part of authentic Mexican folk painting, free from foreign influence, simple, naive, primitive: the natural expression of the purest feeling of the common man."

Fittingly Father Alfaro is interred in a wall near the altar. Nearby, on the right aisle in a glass case is an icon of Christ called "El Señor de la Columna." The statue, among the most venerated in Mexico, is carried during an all-night pilgrimage to the church of San Juan de Dios in San Miguel a few weeks before Easter, and subsequently displayed at several other churches in town before being carried back some weeks later.

Every year a fundamentalist sect of worshippers takes part in flagellation ceremonies for penitents. Although the Church has officially discouraged this custom, it continues at Atotonilco. In an attempt to prevent the worst excesses, however, priests and nuns are assigned to supervise the (mostly private) ceremonies. The annual pilgrimage takes place on the third Sunday in July and draws pilgrims from all parts of the state of Guanajuato, many in their native dress. There is dancing, music, fireworks, and food, balloons, and candy; even little flagellation whips are sold.

In 1996 World Monuments Watch placed Atotonilco on its list of the world's 100 most important buildings in danger of destruction and in need of restoration. It shares this dubious distinction with the Taj Mahal.

PHOTOGRAPHS

*Mexican churches so often have that slightly lopsided, mildly deranged look;
they were clearly made by striving, imperfect, talented, but fallible
human beings, which may account for some of their strong appeal.*

- Alice Adams
Mexico: Some Travels and Some Travelers There

La Parroquia de San Miguel Arcángel

La Parroquia de San Miguel Arcángel

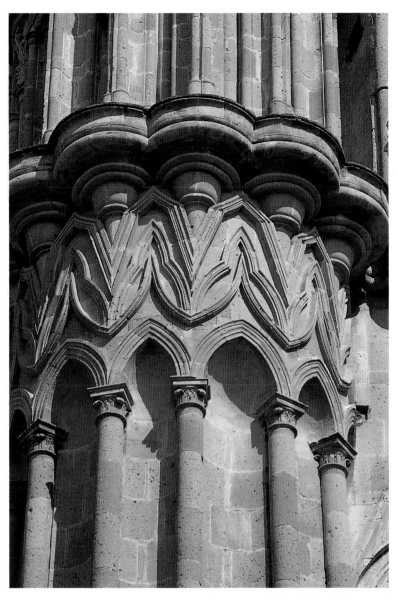

La Parroquia de San Miguel Arcángel

La Iglesia de San Rafael or La Santa Escuela de Cristo

El Templo de la Tercera Orden

La Iglesia de San Francisco

La Iglesia de San Francisco

La Iglesia y Convento de la Concepción

La Iglesia y Convento de la Concepción

La Iglesia de Santo Domingo

El Oratorio de San Felipe Neri

El Templo de San Juan de Dios

La Capilla de la Cañada de Atascadero

La Capilla de La Palmita

La Parroquia de San Antonio

La Iglesia de La Estación

San Miguel Viejo

San Miguel Viejo

Guerrero II

San Miguelito I

Marroquín de Abajo I

Flores de Begonia

Atotonilco

Agustín González II

Agustín González IV

Agustín González IV

Cabrera

Palo Colorado

Montecillo de Nieto III

Montecillo de Nieto III

Providencia de Soasnabar

Palo Verde

Bandita I

El Cortijo

63

La Petaca

Banda I

Don Francisco

Cruz del Palmar

Cruz del Palmar

Cruz del Palmar

Peña Blanca

Santas Marías

Xotolar

San Lucas

El Espejo I

Fajardo de Támbula

La Biznaga de Jaral

San Francisco Xavier

Salitrillo I

Los Ricos de Abajo III

Soria II

Los Martínez

Los Rodríguez

La Palmita

Jesús María La Petaca

Las Cañas II   San Martín El Paredón

Puerta del Aire   Pozo de Balderas

Puerto de Nieto

APPENDIX

The following is an alphabetized list of nearly 300 churches and chapels, new and old, abandoned and active, private and public, scattered throughout the municipio of San Miguel de Allende. Except for St. Paul's Episcopal Church, all the religious buildings in active use belong to the Roman Catholic Church. The notation "under construction" does not mean that religious services are not being held; rather, that the building itself is not finished: it may lack walls, a door, even a roof, and that condition, always due to lack of funds, may have been in effect for years, even decades. "Private" means that religious services are not normally held, and that the building is privately owned. In many cases those chapels are used as residences, as barns for livestock, or as storage buildings. The absence of the word "private" does not, however, mean that the chapel is not privately owned; ascertaining ownership was often not possible. "Abandoned" means that no effort seems to be expended to use the building in any utilitarian way, and that no maintenance is being performed. "In ruins" means that although the structure will be readily recognized as having once been a chapel, all hope for saving it is lost.

In the Town of San Miguel de Allende

The well-known churches in or near the historic center of San Miguel are listed by their proper names, lesser-known churches by the neighborhood in which they are located. When the building or the location is obscure, a specific address is given.

Calvario, El
Cañada de Atascadero, La; in ruins
Chepitos, Los; private, in ruins
Concepción, Iglesia y Convento de la
Cruz del Pueblo, private, Cuesta de Loreto 8
Cuevitas I, Las
Cuevitas II, Las
Ermita, La, de Nuestra Señora de Loreto
Estación, La; Calzada de la Estación
Guadalupe, Capilla de
Guadiana, Capilla de
Instituto Allende; private
Loreto, Santa Casa de; *see* San Felipe Neri

Luz, La; under construction
Malanquin; under construction
Monjas, Las; *see* Concepción
Nuevo Pantoja; under construction
Obraje, Capilla del
Ojo de Agua, Capilla del
Oratorio; *see* San Felipe Neri
Palmita I, La; Cuesta de Loreto
Palmita II, La; private, Salida a Querétaro 90
Palmita III, La; private, in ruins, Salida a
  Querétaro 76
Parroquia, La; *see* San Miguel Arcángel
St. Paul's Episcopal Church

Salud, Templo de Nuestra Señora de la
San Antonio, Templo de
San Felipe Neri, Oratorio de, y Santa Casa de
  Loreto
San Francisco, Iglesia de
San José, Capilla de
San Juan de Dios, Templo de
San Miguel Arcángel, Parroquia de
San Rafael, Templo de; *see* Santa Escuela
San Rafael, Capilla de
Santa Ana, Iglesia de

Santa Cruz del Chorro, Capilla de la
Santa Escuela de Cristo; *see* San Rafael
Santa Julia, Capilla de
Santo Domingo, Iglesia de
Santuario Hogar Mexiquito; Aurora
Señor de la Piedad, Capilla del; private, Calle
  Organos 50
Siete Dolores de la Santísima Virgen, Oratorio
  de los; in ruins, Calle Piedras Chinas
Tercera Orden, Templo de la
Valle del Maíz, Capilla del

In the Countryside of San Miguel de Allende

The chapels in the ranchos in the municipality of San Miguel are listed by location only; the repetition of many of the names by which the chapels are known locally (Virgen de Guadalupe, San Isidro, Santa Cruz, etc.) is numbing and, for purposes of identification, confusing. Too, the names of most of the abandoned chapels have been lost, a troubling but regular occurrence in a culture with mostly oral traditions.

Also listed is a *calvario* in Cruz del Palmar. Usually calvarios are tiny, doorless niches situated within the atrium of a church, decorated with crosses, floral offerings, and burning candles. However, the calvario in Cruz del Palmar is unusual. It is quite large, has a door, and to the casual visitor appears to be a little chapel, which it most certainly is not (mass is not served, there is no bell). Still, villagers sometimes refer to it as a capillita, a little chapel. Since it was built on a pyramid-shaped hill, some people assume that it was erected atop an Aztec temple. Not true.

When there is more than one chapel in a village, the main or active church is indicated as Roman numeral (I). Other chapels in the same community are labelled in Roman numerals as well, with the lower number indicating greater proximity to the main church, i.e. (III) is closer to the main house of worship than (IV). Not even the most detailed map could show the location of some of the chapels, and the simplified map reproduced here can only hint at the places where these structures can be found. The letter abbreviations refer to the location of the chapels relative to the nearest roads as indicated on the map: (Q) road to Querétaro; (DH) road to Dolores Hidalgo; (DM) road to Dr. Mora; (C) road to Celaya; (G) road to Guanajuato; (J) road to Jalpa; (JR) road to Juventino Rosas; (CO) road to Corral de Piedras de Arriba; (CP) road to Cruz del Palmar, which can be reached via the Guanajuato Road, or—in the dry season only—via the Dolores Hidalgo Road.

Agustín González I (G) under construction
Agustín González II (G) abandoned
Agustín González III (G) in ruins
Agustín González IV (G) in ruins, usually
   underwater
Alcocer (Q)
Alonzo Yáñez (G)
Angostura, La (G)
Aparicio (DM) private
Atotonilco, Santuario de (DH)
Atotonilco, Monasterio Benedictino (DH)
Banda I (CP)
Banda II (CP) private
Banda III (CP) private
Bandita (CP)
Begonia del Progreso (G)
Barrones, Los (DH)
Biznaga de Cerro Grande, La (DM)
Biznaga del Jaral, La (J)
Boca de la Cañada I (G)
Boca de la Cañada II (G) private
Bocas (Q)
Cabras (C) also known as Don Juan Xido and
   as Cañada de Begoña
Cabrera (DM)
Calderón (C)
Calera, La (CO)
Campana, La (J)
Cañada de la Virgen, La (G) in ruins
Cañada de los Flores, La (DM)
Cañajo I (Q)
Cañajo II (Q) private
Cañas I, Las (DH)
Cañas II, Las (DH) abandoned
Capadero, El (DH) under construction
Capilla Blanca (DH)
Carmen, El (DM) under construction
Cedro I, El (CP) private, abandoned
Cedro II, El (CP) private, abandoned
Cedro III, El CP) private, in ruins
Cerrito de los Chávez, El (DM) under
   construction
Cerritos (Q)
Charco Azul (G) abandoned
Charco de Sierra , El (J) under construction
Ciénega de Juana Ruiz I, La (G)
Ciénega de Juana Ruiz II, La (G) private,
   abandoned
Ciénega de Juana Ruiz III, La (G) private,
   abandoned
Ciénega de Juana Ruiz IV, La (G) private,
   abandoned
Cieneguita I, La (DH)

Cieneguita II, La (DH) private
Cieneguita III, La (DH) private
Cimatario, El (JR)
Cinco Señores (G)
Clavellinas (CO)
Colorado, El (CO)
Corral de Piedras de Abajo (G)
Corral de Piedras de Arriba (CO)
Corralejo de Arriba (Q)
Corralejo de Abajo (G)
Cortijo, El (DH) private, abandoned
Cruz del Palmar I (CP)
Cruz del Palmar II (CP) private
Cruz del Palmar III (CP) private
Cruz del Palmar IV (CP) private
Cruz del Palmar V (CP) calvario
Cuadrilla de la Petaca I, La (DH)
Cuadrilla de la Petaca II, La (DH) abandoned
Doña Juana (J)
Don Francisco (G)
Don Juan (G) under construction
Don Juan Xido, *see* Cabras
Elvira (J)
Embargo, El (JR) under construction
Espejo I, El (G)
Espejo II, El (G) in ruins
Esquina, La (J)
Estancia de Canal, La (C)
Estancia de San Antonio, La (DM)
Fajardo de Támbula (Q)
Flores de Begonia I (C)
Flores de Begonia II (C)
Flores de Begonia III (C) private, abandoned
Fraile, El (DM) under construction
Frailes, Los (C)
Galvanes I, Los (DH) under construction
Galvanes II, Los (DH) abandoned
Girasol, El (DH)
González, Los (DM) under construction
Guadalupe de Canal (Q)
Guadalupe de la Luz (DM) under construction
Guadalupe de Támbula (Q)
Guadianilla I (G)
Guadianilla II (G) private
Guanajuatito (Q)
Guerrero I (CP) under construction
Guerrero II (CP) private, abandoned
Guerrero III (CP)
Guerreros I, Los (DH)
Guerreros II, Los (DH) private
Guías, Los (DH)
Huerta I, La (G)
Huerta II, La (G) private

Huerta III, La (G) private, abandoned
Huizachal, El (Q)
Jacales, Los (DM) abandoned
Jalpa (J)
Jesús María la Petaca I (DM)
Jesús María la Petaca II (DM) abandoned
Jovero, El (DM)
Juan González I (G)
Juan González II (G) abandoned
Juárez, Los (DH)
Laguna Escondida, La (CO)
Lagunilla, La (J)
Landeta I (DM) under construction
Landeta II (DM) private)
Lejona, La (C) private
Loma de la Purísima (DM) under construction
Loma de las Cocinas (DM) under construction
López, Los (DH)
Luz, La (G) under construction
Manantiales (G)
Marroquín de Abajo I (DH)
Marroquín de Abajo II (DH) abandoned
Marroquín de Arriba (DM) private
Martínez, Los (G)
Medina, La (DM)
Membrillo, El (J) under construction
Montecillo de la Milpa I (DH) under
    construction
Montecillo de la Milpa II (DH) private
Montecillo de la Milpa III (DH) abandoned
Montecillo de la Milpa IV (DH) private
Montecillo de Nieto I (DH)
Montecillo de Nieto II (DH) abandoned
Montecillo de Nieto III (DH) in ruins
Moral de Puerto de Nieto, El (Q)
Moral de Puerto de Sosa, El (DM)
Oaxaca I (CP)
Oaxaca II (CP) abandoned
Ojo de Agua (CP) private
Organos, Los (DM) under construction
Palma, La (DH)
Palmilla, La (DH) under construction
Palmita, La (J)
Palmita, La (G)
Palo Blanco (J) under construction
Palo Colorado (DH)
Palo Verde (G) private, abandoned
Pedregal de Jericó (CO) under construction
Peña Blanca (G)
Peñón de los Baños, El (DM) under
    construction
Perla, La (DM)
Petaca, La (DH) private

Playa, La (DM) under construction
Pozo de Balderas (DH)
Presa Ignacio Allende I (G)
Presa Ignacio Allende II (G)
Presa de la Cantera (C) under construction
Providencia de Soasnabar, La (J) under
    construction
Puente del Carmen (Q)
Puerta del Aire (J) under construction
Puerto de Calderón (C) private
Puerto de Nieto (Q)
Puerto de Sosa I (DM)
Puerto de Sosa II (DM) private
Rancho Viejo I (DH)
Rancho Viejo II (DH) private
Rancho Viejo III (DH) private
Rancho Viejo IV (DH) private
Reyes, Los (CO) under construction
Ricos de Arriba, Los (Q)
Ricos de Abajo I, Los (DH)
Ricos de Abajo II, Los (DH) private
Ricos de Abajo III, Los (DH) private
Rincón de Canal (C)
Rodríguez I, Los (DM)
Rodríguez II, Los (DM)
Salitre, El (G)
Salitrillo 1 (G) near Presa de Allende
Salitrillo 2, I (G) near Soria, private, abandoned
Salitrillo 2, II (G) near Soria, in ruins
Salto de los Galvanes (DH)
San Antonio de la Joya (G)
San Antonio del Plan (DM)
San Antonio del Varal (Q)
San Cristóbal (DM)
San Damián I (G)
San Damián II (G)
San Francisco I (DH) abandoned
San Francisco II (DH) in ruins
San Francisco III (DH) in ruins
San Francisco Xavier (CO)
San Isidro de Bandita (CP)
San Isidro de la Cañada (G)
San Isidro El Capadero I (CP)
San Isidro El Capadero II (CP)
San Isidro El Capadero III (CP) private
San Isidro El Capadero IV (CP) private
San José de Gracia (DM)
San José de la Palma (Q) under construction
San José de Allende (JR) under construction
San José de las Viborillas (DM) under
    construction
San Julián (DM)
San Luis Rey (DH) under construction

San Lucas (G)
San Marcos (G)
San Martín del Paredón I (DM)
San Martín del Paredón II (DM) private
San Martín de la Petaca (DH) under
  construction
San Miguel Viejo (one mile west of railroad
  station)
San Miguelito I (DH) near Atotonilco
San Miguelito II (DH) near Atotonilco
San Miguelito (DM) near Los Rodríguez
San Rafael (CO)
Santa Fe (DM)
Santa Rita (JR) under construction
Santas Marías I (Q)
Santas Marías II (Q)
Santa Teresita de Don Diego (C)
San Valente (DM) under construction
Soasnabar (J)
Soria I (G)
Soria II (G)

Taboada (DH) private, abandoned
Talega, La (DM)
Tierra Blanca de Abajo I (CP)
Tierra Blanca de Abajo II (CP)
Tierra Blanca de Abajo III (CP) abandoned
Tierra Blanca de Arriba (DH)
Tigre, El (J)
Tinaja, La (G)
Tinaja de los Rodríguez, La (J)
Tlaxcalilla I (G)
Tlaxcalilla II (G) in ruins
Toriles, Los (JR)
Torres, Los (CP) private
Tovares, Los (G)
Tres Palmas (DM)
Trojes de Belén, Los (DH)
Trojes del Nombre de Dios, Los (G)
Valle, Los (G) abandoned
Vergel de los Laureles (DH)
Vivienda de Arriba, La (CP)
Xotolar (G) under construction

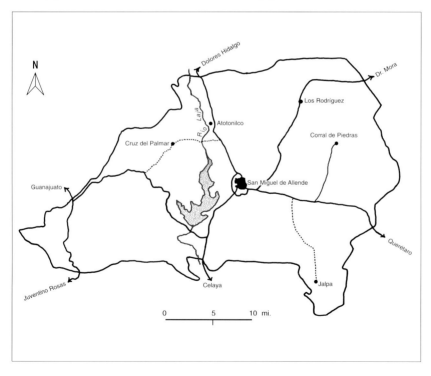